W9-CAL-663

tell

someone worth kiss

THIS BOOK BELONGS TO

_____

GIVEN WITH KISSES BY

_____

ON

our eyes locked

kiss

passionate

XOXO

KISS & TELL

CONCEIVED AND EDITED BY
Cabell Harris

COMPILED BY
Macy's

WITH CONTRIBUTIONS BY (IN ORDER OF APPEARANCE):
Katie Couric • Venus Williams • Elizabeth Banks • Marg Helgenberger • Nicole Miller • Giuliana DePandi
Jamie-Lynn Sigler • Monique Lhuillier • Lisa Rinna • Melania Trump • Wendy Williams • Nicky Hilton
Fran Drescher • Summer Sanders • Kimora Lee Simmons • Amerie • Vanessa Minnillo • Cynthia Steffe
Rozanda "Chilli" Thomas • Olivia d'Abo • Sharon Lawrence • Dana Buchman • Poppy Montgomery
Nanette Lepore • Michelle Trachtenberg • Cynthia Rowley • Paris Hilton • Elisabeth Röhm
Brittny Gastineau • Daisy Fuentes • Illeana Douglas • Rachel Roy • Rebecca Moses • Jessica Alba
Shanna Moakler • Gabrielle Union • Joss Stone • Lisa Gastineau • Petra Nemcova • Tamara Tunie
Kelly Ripa • Jane Seymour • Shar Jackson • Betsey Johnson • Kimberly Stewart
Shoshanna Lonstein Gruss • Tara Reid • Alice Roi • Fergie • Donna Karan • Pink

CHRONICLE BOOKS
SAN FRANCISCO

COPYRIGHT © 2006 MACY'S DEPARTMENT STORES, INC., AND WORK LABS
ALL RIGHTS RESERVED. NO PART OF THIS BOOK MAY BE REPRODUCED IN
ANY FORM WITHOUT WRITTEN PERMISSION FROM THE PUBLISHER.

ISBN-10: 0-8118-5791-3
ISBN-13: 978-0-8118-5791-8

MANUFACTURED IN CHINA

CREATIVE DIRECTION:
Cabell Harris

BOOK AND COVER DESIGN:
**Werner Design Werks, Inc.
Minneapolis, Minnesota**

DISTRIBUTED BY MACY'S
NEW YORK, NEW YORK
WEBSITE: MACYS.COM

10 9 8 7 6 5 4 3 2 1

CHRONICLE BOOKS
680 SECOND STREET, SAN FRANCISCO, CALIFORNIA 94107

WWW.CHRONICLEBOOKS.COM

WORK LABS **WORK** APPROVED

During a kiss,
the heart can
sometimes beat
twice as fast
as normal.

Keep kissing.

IF YOU'RE LUCKY,
you have a kiss or two worth remembering.
Maybe it was a quick peck on the dance floor
back in middle school. Or a passionate kiss
on the beach under the moon.
Or even a sloppy kiss from a two-year-old
as you put him down for a nap.

Wherever it was, whenever it was, chances are that kiss changed you
for the better. Because every good kiss (and even the occasional bad one)
reminds you that you're human. That you're not in this life alone.
And most important, that you're someone worth kissing.
Which is a wonderful thing to be, when you really think about it.

In this little book, we've collected kisses—and some terrific stories—
from some of the world's most interesting women. From stars to
socialites, from artists to activists, these ladies have decided to share some
of the kisses that helped make them who they are today.

In a world where far too many people are using their mouths for shouting, it
is our humble wish that this book will help remind people that there are
better things our lips can do.

XOXO

THE EDITORS

KISS & TELL

KATIE
COURIC

I WAS IN SEVENTH GRADE
attending my first girl-boy party ever,
and of course one of the major activities was
spin the bottle. First up was
Joe Wilson, who was real cute.
I had never played spin the bottle before
and I was just praying it wouldn't land on me...

**but of course
my greatest adolescent
nightmare came true**

as the bottle slowly stopped,
pointing in my direction!
I didn't know whether I was
supposed to kiss him
on the mouth or on the cheek.
Terrified of making a complete fool
out of myself, I split the difference.
Needless to say, my first kiss was
very stressful and not very romantic.

xoxoxo!
Katie Couric

VENUS
WILLIAMS

ONE OF MY MOST MEMORABLE EXPERIENCES
is the first time I kissed a newborn baby.
They are so fresh, innocent, and precious.
You can only kiss them for one reason...to give
them love. And the love is unconditional.

ONE OF MY MOST MEMORABLE KISSES happened behind the cinema center in 1987. I was awkward and skinny with a bad perm. There was a group of us and we were pairing off. Nobody had any experience, and we all felt dared, pressured, but excited too. Finally, I kissed a cute, awkward boy.

ELIZABETH
BANKS

A FEW YEARS AGO I stepped into an elevator in Toronto and came face-to-face with a very cute young man, who then proceeded to tell me that I was his first kiss. Flattered though I was, I was somewhat embarrassed as I couldn't recall having shared a kiss with him. He went on to explain that the kiss happened when he was eleven years old while in character as a boy smitten with a grown woman in the movie *Crooked Hearts.* That cute young man in the elevator was Joshua Jackson. I'm honored to have been his first kiss and that it was memorable for him.

MARG
HELGENBERGER

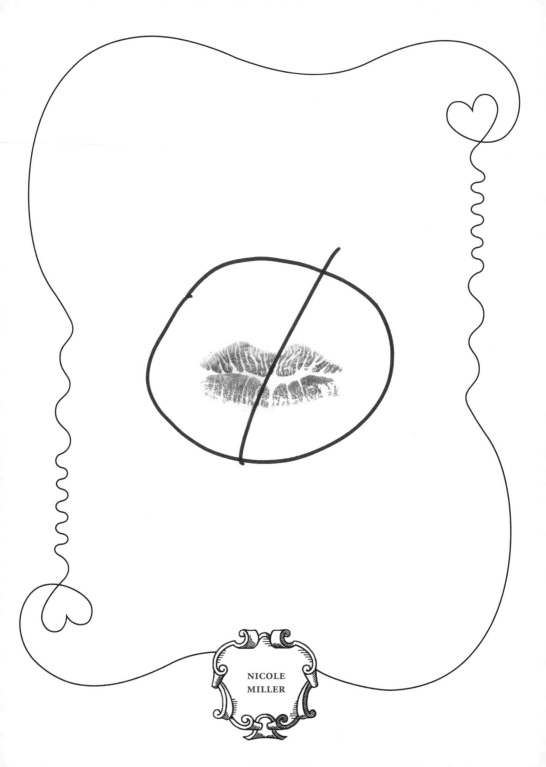

MY SON PALMER has never liked kissing or being kissed. I teased him that after he went to sleep at night I would sneak in and give him kisses. One night when I went in to check on him I found him sleeping with a sign on his chest that said **"No Kissing–No Kissing–No Kissing."**

Nicole Miller

THE BEST KISS IN THE WORLD is the kiss I get from my nieces. You know when they kiss me it's like pure love, and it's so sweet and gentle. There's no kind of intentions, there's no agenda. It's genuine and I feel loved.

XO Giuliana DePandi

GIULIANA
DEPANDI

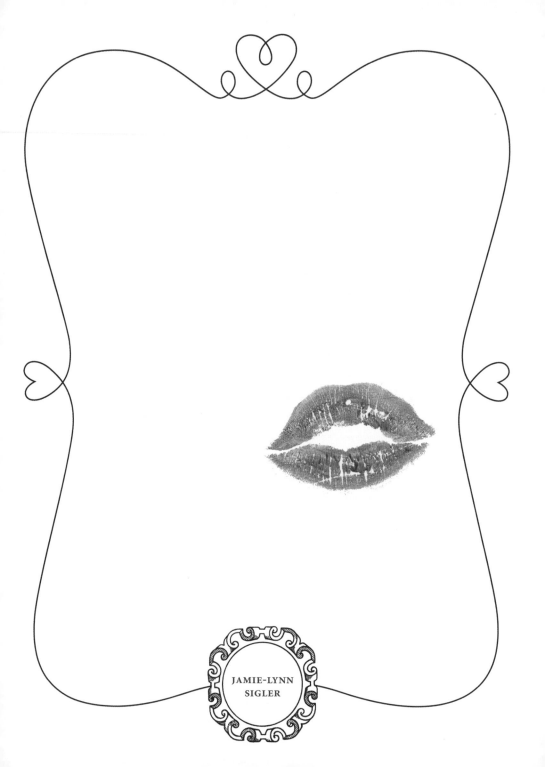

JAMIE-LYNN
SIGLER

MY FIRST KISS **was in the fifth grade.** I was watching *Beverly Hills 90210* with my first boyfriend, Brian Kelly. It was the episode where Brenda and Dylan kissed for the first time, and my boyfriend turned to me and said, "Do you want to kiss like Brenda and Dylan?" And we did. **I remember he tasted like Wildberry Skittles.**

Jennie Lynn Segler

MONIQUE
LHUILLIER

THE DAY MY BABY JACK was born...
All I could think about was this precious little life in
my arms and how I was going to
smother him with kisses.

Monique Lhuillier

My heart belongs to Harry. Every kiss that I give to my husband, every single day, is MY MOST MEMORABLE KISS.

LISA
RINNA

Kisses can be
remembered for
a long time.
Kisses can be platonic,
or they can be
romantic, passionate,
playful, sexy…

A KISS CAN BE MONUMENTAL.

Melania Trump

WENDY
WILLIAMS

MY MOST MEMORABLE KISS had to be my first kiss with my husband. We have been married for seven years, but we have been together instantaneously since our first date. That was 11 years ago. Our date started when I walked downstairs from the radio station. From the radio station we drove in his car to Brooklyn, closed up his hair shop, went by his apartment, and we had great conversation. Next-level conversation.

I think—well, I know—that our first date was supposed to give him bragging rights because he was going out with Wendy from the radio. He was from the other side of the tracks, and I was the big-mouth bitch from the radio. In a way, I guess we were both experiments for each other. Before we even got to the bridge, I knew I really liked him. I liked his conversation, and I saw that he took time for particular things for our first date. I noticed that his outfit was brand-new and crisp. For me, I wore my skinny jeans: a pair of Levi's that held everything in and gave me some butt definition. I liked him, and I felt as though I didn't have to put on pretenses with him. I could be honest with him, and he was very honest with me.

I think what he expected from me was some highfalutin, "Let's go eat lobster at the Rainbow Room," or whatever. But really, I just got in the car and was like, "Okay, what are we going to do?" So we went all through Brooklyn, and then we went to Jersey City, by the water, to eat. We went out for dinner at a very simple place called Houlihan's, and we sat and drank Heineken right out of the bottle—no glass or anything like that. All that took him back because the date didn't cost him more than a few bucks.

Afterward, I brought him back to my apartment. At that time it was maybe eight hours into our date. We did not sleep together that night, but we did do a lot of kissing! It was so easy to fall for his kiss. I had never felt a kiss like that before, and I never concentrated so much on a kiss. Kissing to me is more intimate than having sex, and his kisses were very, very sensual. And I remember thinking, "Wow! He's a better kisser than me!" His kisses were so great. The idea that we spent so much time kissing, not fondling, was great. I was very conscious of my body, and my folds, and things like that. The big girls understand what I am saying. But we have been together ever since and

I consider that kiss to be the beginning of the rest of my life.

MY FIRST KISS was in high school. I had no idea what I was doing—clearly he didn't either. **He slobbered all over me!** I was traumatized for a while. It's my most memorable kiss, but definitely not the greatest.

♡ Nicky Hilton

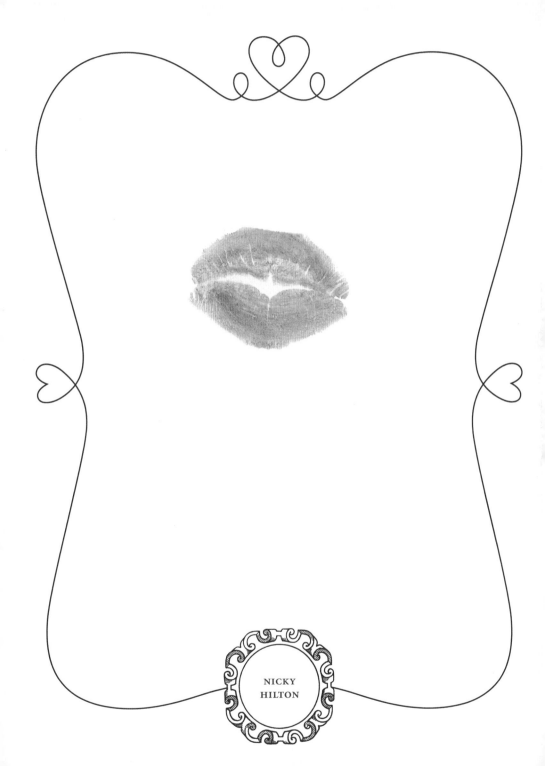

NICKY
HILTON

FRAN
DRESCHER

IT WAS 1970 in Spring Valley, New York. I can remember like it was yesterday. My sister and I were visiting our older cousin Ira for the weekend. Ira was going to the Fireman's Carnival with his friends, and me and Nadine were invited to join. I didn't know what to wear, but I knew I wanted to look cool and thin and older. I ended up with a brown-felt floppy hat, a tank top, and jeans with sandals. Ira's friends were around three years older than I, and all were cute to me and my sister. There were rides and game booths everywhere, and then there was Allan Ginsberg. We started going on all the rides together, then walking hand in hand. He said I looked pretty. He said he was glad I came, and he was having a lot of fun. I said I was glad I came and was having fun, too. Then Allan Ginsberg leaned over and kissed me gently, softly on the lips and said, "Thank you…"

Fran Dreocher

SUMMER
SANDERS

MY MOST MEMORABLE KISS STORY
is about my first-ever blind date.
It was November 6, 2003. I was so nervous before the date.
What should I wear? What should I do when I meet him? Should I
shake his hand, kiss his cheek, or hug him? I decided to kiss him
on the cheek. Later I learned that was his strategy as well. That kiss
started off the best date of my life. His name is Erik Schlopy,

and he is now my husband!

THERE IS NOTHING LIKE the first kiss of your newborn child!

Kimora Lee Simmons

KIMORA
LEE
SIMMONS

I WAS SO NERVOUS about the kiss I had to do for the movie *First Daughter.* I was sitting down next to Katie Holmes when the guy I had to kiss came in for rehearsals. Suddenly, I started crying uncontrollably from embarrassment, and I hid my face behind Katie's shoulder. I didn't want to be unprofessional, so I did eventually pull myself together. :)

AMERIE

I KNEW IT WAS A SPECIAL KISS when he leaned in and gently kissed my lips, then said, "You have nice *labios*." I said, "What?" He said, "Lips." We kissed again and he literally took my breath away. They say, you know when you know… I knew and never forgot that kiss.

Vanessa Minnillo

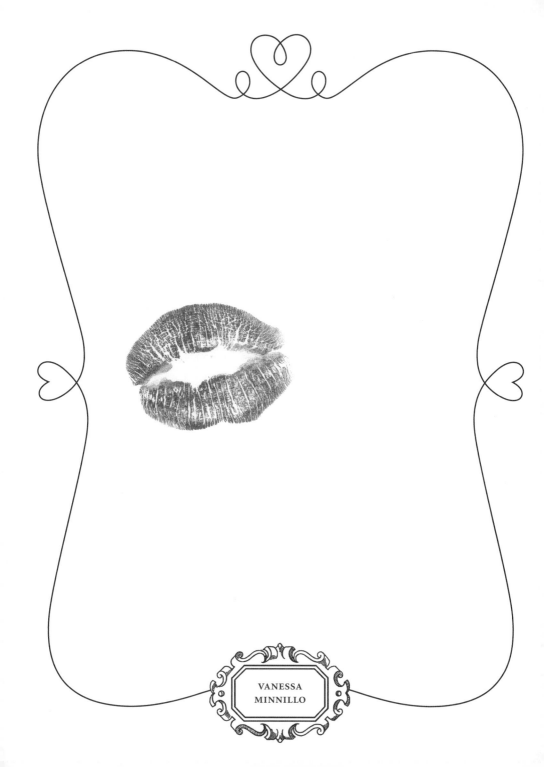

VANESSA
MINNILLO

CYNTHIA
STEFFE

ONE OF MY MOST MEMORABLE
and surprising kisses came from my
daughter Ava, when she was not quite
a year old. Of course, I had given her
plenty of kisses, but this time she planted
one on me. She reached out and firmly
placed her two small hands on my cheeks,
turning my face so that she was looking
directly into my eyes, then leaned in. I
was caught completely off guard, and
I felt it to the core of my heart.

Cynthia Steffe

MY FIRST AND MOST PRECIOUS KISS
was the moment I laid eyes on my son Tron and
kissed him smack on the lips, over and over again.
That was truly my first kiss.

ROZANDA
"CHILLI"
THOMAS

OLIVIA
D'ABO

I was about twelve or thirteen

and lived in Taos, New Mexico, at the time.
I had a huge crush on a boy called Jeff Yoman.

He was dreamy.

I'd been away in Los Angeles and had just come
back home after the end of summer.
A bunch of friends sat around and played truth or dare,
and Jeff and I sat together in the circle.
My friend Bliss dared Jeff to kiss me,
and I was shaking because
I didn't know how to kiss back!
He turned to me with a huge grin on his face
and said, "Finally! Yikes!"
He touched my face and then
planted one straight on me…
somehow he led me through it
and I just tried to breathe.
It was gentle, beautiful, and very long.

That was my first kiss,

AND I'LL NEVER FORGET IT.

Olivia d'Abo

WHEN I STAND SO CLOSE TO HIM, I feel the heat coming off his body and my own temperature rises. When I feel the bubble in my belly fill with pastel pebbles tumbling and tickling me from the inside. When I hear only the rhythm of my pulsing blood as it gains momentum through my body—when I smell his scent as it wraps around mine—when he shares the breath between us—when time stops the moment before we kiss—it is as sweet as the kiss itself.

Sharon Lawrence

SHARON
LAWRENCE

WHEN I SAW TOM ACROSS THE ROOM
at a smoky, loud party in 1987, I knew I wanted to kiss him. And when we kissed later that night, in a quiet back room far from the dancing and the crowd, I knew it would be the last time I kissed anyone but him.

Dana Buchman

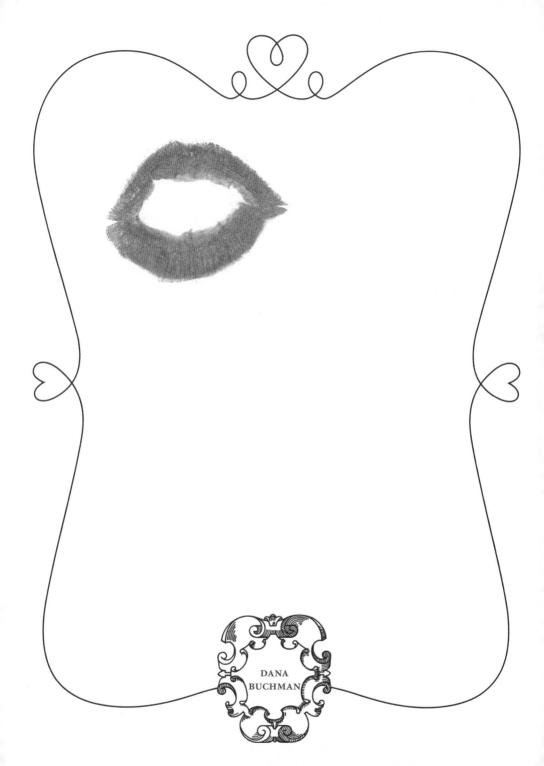

DANA
BUCHMAN

IT IS DIFFICULT TO WRITE about ONE memorable kiss. To me, all kisses are memorable (sometimes the bad ones more than the good). As it's said about pictures, kisses are worth a thousand words. Words will fail to do justice when a kiss won't let you down:

"I love you."

"I want you."

"Don't go."

"I've missed you."

"I'm sorry."

"Sleep well."

"You are everything to me."

You can even give someone a "kiss-off," if need be. It is the best way to tease and tempt, or leave yourself totally vulnerable. The kiss is one of humankind's perfect creations.

Poppy Montgomery

POPPY
MONTGOMERY

NANETTE
LEPORE

kiss and tell!

Nanette Lepore

MICHELLE
TRACHTENBERG

WHEN I WAS SIX YEARS OLD, my best friend dared my
crush to kiss me on the playground.
After some convincing, he did,
but then told all of his friends that I had girl cooties!

Xo

There are some things that should be done
in life and love, and we think
kissing someone in a worthy place tops both lists.
The hopeless romantic–approved destinations
compiled here have won over hundreds of new hearts,
and reignited thousands of old flames.
Yes, countless lovers have come before you,
and countless more will surely come after.
But the memory of the perfect kiss in the perfect place
will always be yours to share with one lucky someone.
And there's even hope for those of us
who can't make the trip: just pucker up
and keep your eyes closed.
IMAGINATION CAN TAKE YOU ANYWHERE...

THE Perfect PLACE

PARIS IN SPRINGTIME
remains the brightest jewel in
Love's golden crown, and a kiss atop the
Eiffel Tower can only be described as the
supreme romantic moment for lovers of all ages.
There are 1,710 steps to the top, or, more
conveniently, one elevator.
Purchase your tickets, hold hands, and
squeeze in next to the eager crowd waiting for
their chance to watch the Seine River
recede into a sparkling ribbon below.
As with any venture of the heart,
timing is everything.
An hour before sunset reveals a perfect
panoramic view of the City of Light, and
the perfect moment to lean in
for a kiss...

Paris

EIFFEL TOWER

Location 01

It's impossible to keep Love's feet on the ground,
so sprout your own wings and soar
above Napa's lush vista in a hot-air balloon.
Hop into the wicker basket,
watch as the colored orb inflates to life,
and let your chariot float in California's warm breeze.
Enjoy a glass of red wine (the color of love)
from the lush vineyards below, and feel as warm and
lazy as the drifting clouds keeping you company.
Bluebirds bob and weave their feathered patterns
on the horizon; fields gently touch their
brown and green fingers together;
and hearts grow soft and full in the afternoon haze,
making way for lips to
MOVE CLOSER...

Napa Valley

Niagara Falls.

The natural wonder formed fifty thousand years ago
by a melting ice sheet is still melting hearts and
keeping Love's course running true.
Niagara Falls calls two countries home,
but the Canadian side is where couples can find
the breathtaking view of three falls cascading with
thunderous applause onto the rocks below.
In summer months, rainbows rise from the spray to
sparkle against the mist cloaking the gathered crowds.
Evergreens hold fast to the river's soft shoulders.
Standing against this dramatic backdrop of
rushing water, your heart runs quickly along
the rapids and a single kiss can
SWEEP YOU OFF YOUR FEET...

NAVIGATING LOVE'S WATERWAYS
has never been an easy task, so sometimes it's best
to just relax and enjoy the ride.
There's no better place to steal a kiss than on a
gondola gliding through one of Venice's many canals.
After an afternoon of sipping cappuccinos
in the piazza with the sun glistening off
San Marco's gilded mosaics,
accept a gondolier's offer to weave you through the
ancient city. Curious tourists peek from the
hundreds of bridges overhead,
water gently laps against the boat's bow,
and your reflections come together in the canal's
mirrored face. This is your chance to
get lost in Venice's mysterious spell...

Venice

THE GRAND CANAL

FINDING A QUIET SPOT FOR LOVE
in the City That Never Sleeps isn't always easy.
Luckily, there is a place that can
soften even the toughest of hearts.
In the middle of it all,
an oasis of peacefulness awaits the truly romantic
in New York's Central Park.
Try nestling under a warm blanket on a carriage ride,
watching people stroll by and listening
to the beat of horses' hooves on the pavement.
As the background noise dulls to a hum,
you are aware of only each other.
A perfect time to drift closer together
and experience the power of a great kiss...

Central Park

NEW YORK CITY

CARRIAGE RIDE

Location 05

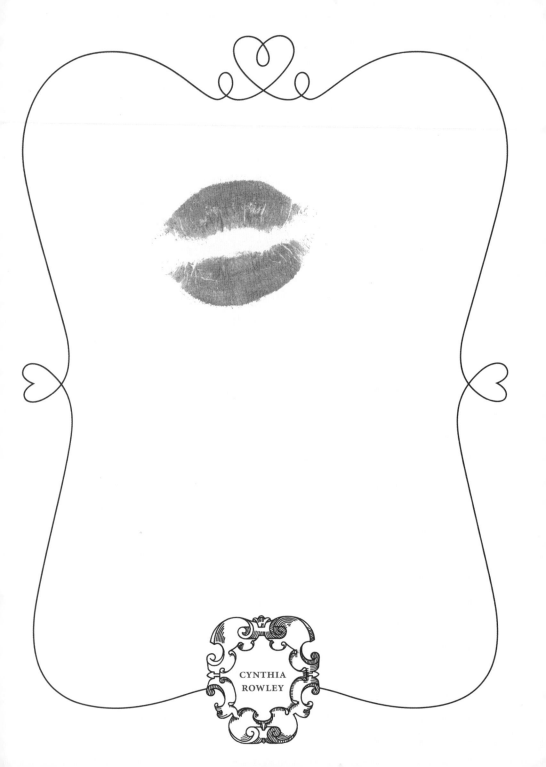

CYNTHIA
ROWLEY

I DID NOT KNOW I was being proposed to.
We were sitting on a bench outside the Taj Mahal.
It was hot, a hundred-plus degrees, sauna hot.
My boyfriend distracts me by asking for the digital camera,
buried in my purse. While I'm searching for it, he says something
romantic along the lines of, "Hey, so I have a question for you." I
look up and he's down on knee, ring in hand,
the Taj's dome framing his idea.

"Will you marry me?"

I answer him with a kiss.

Cynthia Rowley

I think you can tell if you like a guy by the way he kisses. I like a kiss that's soft and sweet. And when you're kissing, a feeling of happiness takes over your body. It's hard to find a good kiss, but when you do, it's amazing. The first time my boyfriend and I kissed was while we were walking through the lobby of the Roosevelt Hotel. We had just started seeing each other and were trying to be discreet. It was so sudden and so exciting, it was the best kiss of my life. I was kissed like I'd never been kissed before. It was

A KISS I WILL NEVER FORGET.

PARIS
HILTON

ELISABETH
RÖHM

MY FIRST KISS EVER was with Jeremy Bernstein, who had to take his retainer out, and it was honestly one of the grossest experiences of my life.

I was at Melissa Wanoker's house who was the star of *Hairspray*, and I think at the time we were probably eleven years old and we were having a party. I think beers were involved. And I think there was one parent there supervising. And they had this big, beautiful property in Bedford, New York, with lots of gardens and waterfalls and bridges. And Jeremy Bernstein leads me to this big bridge in the backyard and says something like, "Let's sit down and talk." So we're sitting there talking, and suddenly he goes and (in this really unsuave manner) takes his index finger and his thumb and pulls out his retainer and pounces on me. Let me assure you, it was the worst sloppy kiss ever, and my first kiss ever.

Elizabeth Röhm

MY MOST MEMORABLE KISS: I went to dinner with my boyfriend about fifteen blocks away from my NYC apartment. On the way home from the restaurant it began pouring rain, a torrential downfall, and we realized we had no money, only credit cards. We had to walk back in the rain, when he began kissing me, and we made out the entire time back to my home. His kisses were romantic and passionate, and I will always remember them.

Brittney Gastineau

BRITTNY
GASTINEAU

MY FIRST KISS...I was in fifth grade. Yes! Fifth.
There was a cute boy...probably the only fifth-grade boy who was into girls and a flirt.
He had a crush on me, but I thought, "Yuck." One day we were doing a group thing
in class, and in front of everyone he got my attention. When I turned to see what he
wanted, he planted one on me. Right on the lips. I chased him around the room until
I caught him and punched him. Thinking back on it today, I think how ballsy I was,
and, yes, secretly—how cute! Should have kissed him back.

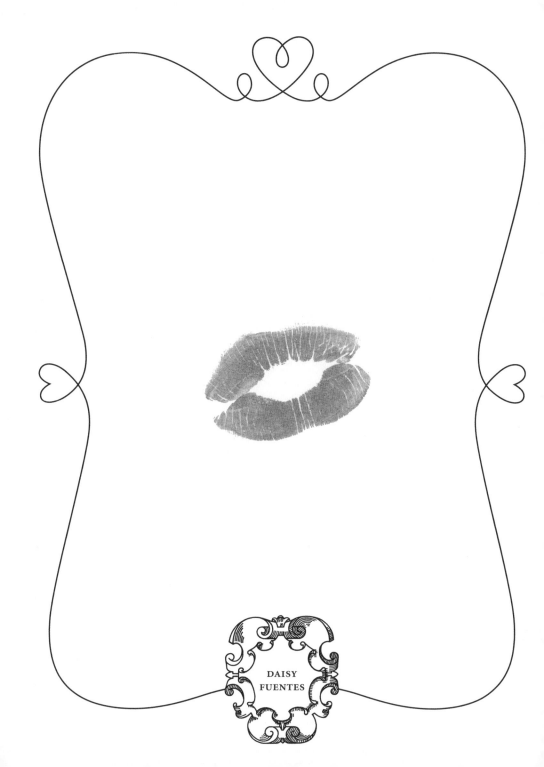

DAISY
FUENTES

ILLEANA
DOUGLAS

MY FIRST KISS WAS **Robby at the top of the slide at the elementary school.**

Illeana Douglas

A kiss from my daughter is the closest thing to knowing heaven I will experience in my lifetime. The perfection of unconditional love, the art of giving and asking for nothing in return is felt when she wakes me up in the morning with sweet kisses on my eyes and sends me to sleep with "Sweet dreams meme" and kisses on my cheek. God offers supreme joy in uncomplicated forms. One of life's serenely sweetest little pleasures is a kiss from my tiny little fairy angel, Ava.

MOMMY LOVES YOU ALWAYS.

Rachel Roy ♡

RACHEL
ROY

KISSING IS THE BEST. **It's pure magic. Heart throbbing, passions rising, butterflies fly madly—that amazing movement when two pairs of lips touch. Oh, the excitement, the fireworks.**

What a "moment"! Let's hope the moment endures and endures. The real passion of romance is symbolized by the first kiss—the better the kissing, the better everything else. When a kiss is done well, it is an art form. One that is so much fun to perfect.

It takes time to perfect kissing. The first kiss, whether done at fourteen or fifty, is felt with such anticipation that at times it can be awkward.

My very first kiss was when I was fourteen years old with N.S. (I don't kiss and tell). He was fourteen, too. We were at my house after school. I remember everything I wore that day. We were sitting on the sofa watching television, and he put his arm around my shoulder and before I knew it our lips were as close as they could be. WOW! I was so awkward at first, but then you sort of get the hang of it and it gets so exciting. I thought: Do I keep my eyes open or closed? They closed pretty quickly. Nature is wonderful. And just while I'm getting the knack of this amazing experience, my older sister walks in. **But how I remember that first kiss. The moment seems to always stay in your heart.**

Rebecca Moses

REBECCA
MOSES

JESSICA
ALBA

KISSES ARE THE BEST WAY
to connect with someone
you really love and care about.

MY FAVORITE KISS is the first kiss I had with my husband! I love it so much because it was awful! And that's what makes it so special; we were so nervous and waited so long to do it. I had never kissed someone with a lip piercing before, so when that magical moment came and we drew closer, we smacked teeth and I hit his metal piercing. We both looked at each other in shock and started laughing. It was actually sweet. I knew right then and there he was the one! Of course, we tried again, this time slower. To this day when I kiss him, I can feel it in my toes!

SHANNA
MOAKLER

MY FIRST KISS

was with a cute boy named Brian, right in front of my grandma's house. We were so nervous and my leg was shaking uncontrollably. When he leaned in to kiss me, I froze. It was so sweet and gentle. I was on cloud nine for weeks.

Gabrielle Union

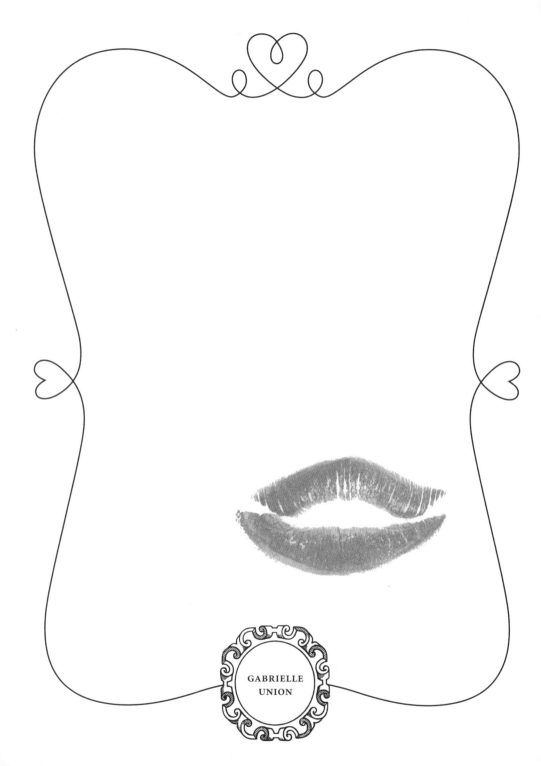

GABRIELLE
UNION

JOSS
STONE

WELL, WHEN YOU'RE YOUNG there's always one boy that all the girls simply do not want to kiss. I can remember sitting in that circle we all know with a bottle spinning in the middle. Every time it landed on this particular boy, whoever the girl was, she would literally (no joke) run screaming from the room. This happened three times. I thought it was cruel. I felt so bad for Mr. XXX that, when it came round to me, of course I kissed him. The girls ripped me for months, and Mr. XXX followed me around for ages. I haven't seen him in years. Serves them all right if he turned into a complete babe!

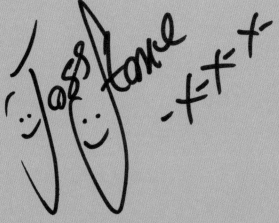

MY FIRST KISS:
Seven minutes in heaven in a coat closet
at my girlfriend's party with my
biggest CRUSH in my whole thirteen years!
I'll never forget the moment...

LISA
GASTINEAU

PETRA
NEMCOVA

THE MOST BEAUTIFUL, PASSIONATE, ROMANTIC KISS

happened on the 2nd of July, 2003. In the park in London. It was Simon's and my first kiss. We were lying on the grass in each other's arms at least half an hour, maybe 45 minutes, our lips together. It was so gentle, passionate, and beautiful. The longest kiss I ever experienced. We opened and closed our eyes, but we never left each other's arms. Our lips stayed locked. I saw people walking by looking at us. And I'm sure they were thinking, "Gross! Go get a room!" Maybe if I weren't part of that kiss, I would have thought the same thing myself. It is impossible to explain the ecstasy of that moment. Lying there on the grass, with the sun coming through the branches of the trees and dappling our cheeks with warmth, hearing the sound of the wind rustling the leaves, hearing the distant voices of children playing, I felt such a sense of peace and happiness. I will never forget it.

MY FAVORITE KISS as a little girl was when my father would come home from work. I'd greet him at the top of the stairs and he'd say, "Who loves me?" And I would say, "I do!" He would then say, "How much?" And I would shout, **"A BUSHEL AND A PECK AND A HUG AROUND THE NECK!"** And I'd fling myself into his arms and throw my arms around his neck, and we'd plant big kisses on each other. And then I'd go back to whatever I was doing. I was a lucky kid!

TAMARA
TUNIE

THE FIRST TIME I KISSED MY HUSBAND was during his screen test for *All My Children.* Although it was very professional and not at all romantic, I knew that he would get the job and that I would marry him!

Kelly Ripa

KELLY
RIPA

MY MOST MEMORABLE KISS was when I was filming a small, romantic movie called *Somewhere in Time.*

We filmed in sequence and built up to the moment when Chris Reeve's character kisses me in a hallway. It was a very romantic moment both on and off screen, and one I will never forget. He was very tall and I was at least a foot shorter–this made it even more romantic.

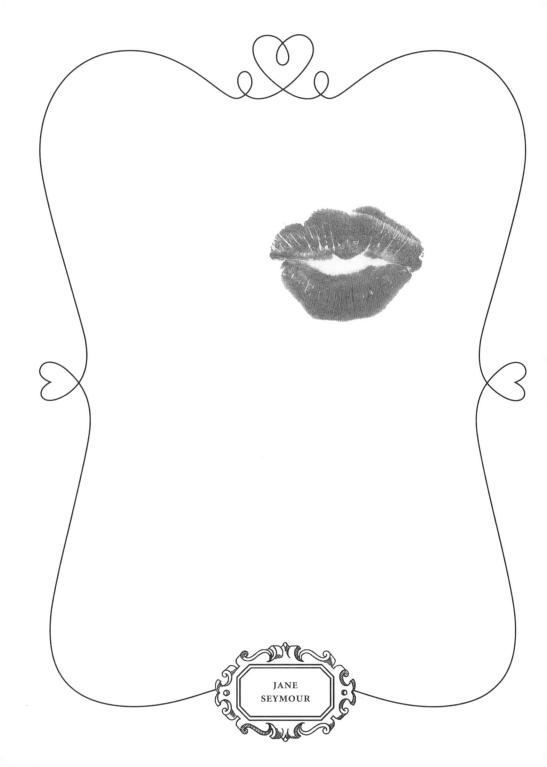

JANE
SEYMOUR

MY MOST MEMORABLE KISS

was caught on camera and put in a magazine…
It was the first kiss to my newborn baby boy.

SHAR
JACKSON

BETSEY
JOHNSON

MY MOST MEMORABLE KISS is the kiss I gave
to my daughter Lulu when I gave her
away down the aisle on her wedding day.

KIMBERLY
STEWART

MY FIRST KISS was when I was sixteen in a movie theater.

SHOSHANNA
LONSTEIN
GRUSS

My husband, Josh, and I were casual acquaintances growing up in New York City. We said hi and made chitchat when we saw each other around town. I always thought he was gorgeous and so sweet.

One night in the fall of 2001 at a mutual friend's birthday party, I saw him from across the room and I was overwhelmed. I thought I would be so lucky if I could kiss that boy. I walked over, said hi, and we started talking. Our conversation lasted all night. Toward the end of the party we were holding hands. Later that night, Josh asked if he could drive me home. Of course, I said yes. He asked for my number as we pulled up to my building. As he was walking me to my door, I was scared he might have taken the phone number down wrong, so I asked for his.

As I was looking down programming his number into my phone, he put his arm around my waist and leaned in for a kiss.

I nearly melted into the sidewalk.
And as they say,

THE REST IS HISTORY.

A KISS IS JUST A KISS,

unless
it's not
just
a kiss.

Tara Reid

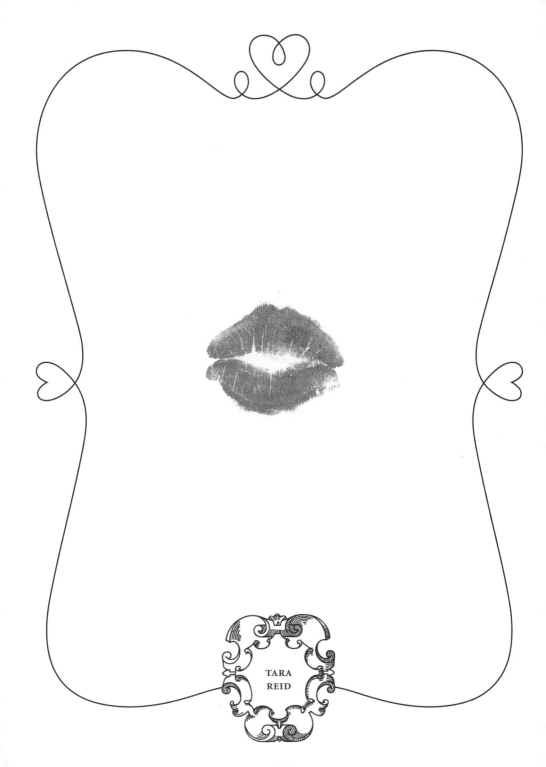

TARA
REID

I HAD MY FIRST KISS during
spin the bottle
at a 1950s theme party. I was wearing a pink

crinoline skirt and saddle shoes.

ALICE
ROI

MY FIRST KISS was at the wrap party for *Kids Incorporated*. It was my puppy love, Ryan Lambert, who was on the show with me. I was eleven and he was fifteen, and then we made out again when he showed me *Sid & Nancy.* No wonder I'm so crazy!

I HAD A CRUSH on a boy in the first grade.
The class was watching a movie on elephants and lions, and I
knew the moment had come. I took off my bandana and used it
for us to hide behind. It was a very private, special kiss.

DONNA
KARAN

PINK

than a sloppy,
unconditional,
and passionate kiss.
From a bulldog.
Named Elvis.

LET'S GET PERSONAL.
Now it's your turn to kiss and tell.

No two kisses are alike.
No two kissers are, either.
The kisses you've given and received are
unique to you and you alone: so use this
section to give them their due.
The good, the bad, and the good-because-they're-bad.
Write them down in all their
lip-smacking, toe-curling glory.

YOUR
LIP PRINT
HERE

DEAR DIARY

KISS & TELL

my most memorable kiss was...

_____

WHO

_____

WHERE

_____

WHEN

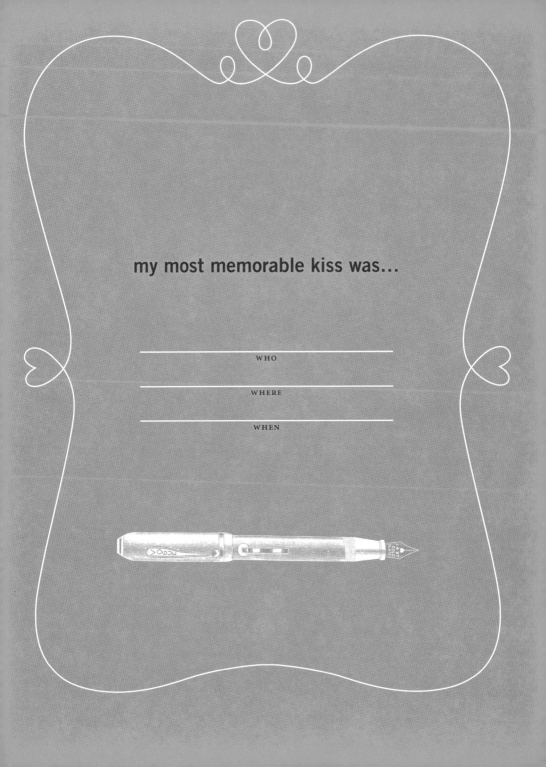

xoxo

_____

_____

_____

_____

_____

_____

_____

_____

_____

_____

_____

_____

_____

_____

_____

_____

_____

_____

XOXO

check off all the places

WHERE YOU HAVE STOLEN A MEMORABLE KISS

In the dark ○   ○ On the 4th of July

At the movies ○   ○ On New Year's Eve

On a sofa ○   ○ In a tree house

Under a waterfall ○   ○ At the altar

In a boat ○   ○ In a car

At a drive-in ○   ○ In a closet

In a hot-air balloon ○   ○ At a party

On the beach ○   ○ On a golf green

Under the stars ○   ○ In an elevator

On a city sidewalk ○   ○ In a camping tent

At an airport ○   ○ On a picnic

On an airplane ○   ○ On a school bus

check off all the places
WHERE YOU HAVE STOLEN A MEMORABLE KISS

In a car wash ○ ○ On a train

In the woods ○ ○ On the subway

On a porch swing ○ ○ In a museum

At the office ○ ○ In a church

On a roller coaster ○ ○ In a hammock

By a campfire ○ ○ In a hot tub

In a thunderstorm ○ ○ Under mistletoe

While cooking ○ ○ Under the bleachers

On roller or ice skates ○ ○ On a bridge

On a horse ○ ○ By a fireplace

On a ski lift ○ ○ In a field of flowers

At a concert ○ ○ On a rooftop

Thank you for kissing and telling...

Jessica Alba ACTRESS

Amerie SINGER

Elizabeth Banks ACTRESS

Dana Buchman FASHION DESIGNER

Katie Couric TV PERSONALITY

Olivia d'Abo ACTRESS

Giuliana DePandi TV HOST

Illeana Douglas ACTRESS

Fran Drescher ACTRESS

Fergie SINGER, BLACK EYED PEAS

Daisy Fuentes MODEL/TV HOST

Brittny Gastineau MODEL/TV PERSONALITY

Lisa Gastineau TV PERSONALITY

Shoshanna Lonstein Gruss FASHION DESIGNER

Marg Helgenberger ACTRESS

Nicky Hilton HANDBAG DESIGNER

Paris Hilton SOCIALITE/TV PERSONALITY

Shar Jackson ACTRESS

Betsey Johnson FASHION DESIGNER

Donna Karan FASHION DESIGNER

Sharon Lawrence ACTRESS

Nanette Lepore FASHION DESIGNER

Monique Lhuillier FASHION DESIGNER

Nicole Miller FASHION DESIGNER

Vanessa Minnillo MTV VJ

Shanna Moakler MODEL/ACTRESS

Poppy Montgomery TV ACTRESS
Rebecca Moses FASHION DESIGNER
Petra Nemcova MODEL
Pink SINGER
Tara Reid ACTRESS
Lisa Rinna ACTRESS
Kelly Ripa TV PERSONALITY
Elisabeth Röhm ACTRESS
Alice Roi FASHION DESIGNER
Cynthia Rowley FASHION DESIGNER
Rachel Roy FASHION DESIGNER
Summer Sanders OLYMPIC SWIMMER/TV PERSONALITY
Jane Seymour ACTRESS
Jamie-Lynn Sigler ACTRESS
Kimora Lee Simmons FASHION DESIGNER
Cynthia Steffe FASHION DESIGNER
Kimberly Stewart SOCIALITE
Joss Stone SINGER
Rozanda "Chilli" Thomas SINGER
Michelle Trachtenberg ACTRESS
Melania Trump MODEL
Tamara Tunie ACTRESS
Gabrielle Union ACTRESS
Venus Williams PROFESSIONAL ATHLETE
Wendy Williams RADIO HOST

Macy's is the proud national sponsor of the
American Heart Association's Go Red for Women Movement.
Profits from *Kiss & Tell* will benefit this campaign.
This book is available exclusively at Macy's.

Go Red For Women is the
American Heart Association's nationwide movement that
celebrates the energy, passion, and power
we have as women to band together and wipe out heart disease.
Thanks to the participation of millions of people
across the country, the color red and the red dress
have become linked with the ability all women have to improve
their heart health and live stronger, longer lives.

Poppy Montgomery TV ACTRESS
Rebecca Moses FASHION DESIGNER
Petra Nemcova MODEL
Pink SINGER
Tara Reid ACTRESS
Lisa Rinna ACTRESS
Kelly Ripa TV PERSONALITY
Elisabeth Röhm ACTRESS
Alice Roi FASHION DESIGNER
Cynthia Rowley FASHION DESIGNER
Rachel Roy FASHION DESIGNER
Summer Sanders OLYMPIC SWIMMER/TV PERSONALITY
Jane Seymour ACTRESS
Jamie-Lynn Sigler ACTRESS
Kimora Lee Simmons FASHION DESIGNER
Cynthia Steffe FASHION DESIGNER
Kimberly Stewart SOCIALITE
Joss Stone SINGER
Rozanda "Chilli" Thomas SINGER
Michelle Trachtenberg ACTRESS
Melania Trump MODEL
Tamara Tunie ACTRESS
Gabrielle Union ACTRESS
Venus Williams PROFESSIONAL ATHLETE
Wendy Williams RADIO HOST

Macy's is the proud national sponsor of the
American Heart Association's Go Red for Women Movement.
Profits from *Kiss & Tell* will benefit this campaign.
This book is available exclusively at Macy's.

Go Red For Women is the
American Heart Association's nationwide movement that
celebrates the energy, passion, and power
we have as women to band together and wipe out heart disease.
Thanks to the participation of millions of people
across the country, the color red and the red dress
have become linked with the ability all women have to improve
their heart health and live stronger, longer lives.

A SPECIAL THANKS GOES OUT TO

Patti Harris, Leah Muhlenfeld, Dave Muhlenfeld,
Robyn Gunn, and Pem Carter at WORK Labs

•

Sharon Werner and Sarah Nelson at Werner Design Werks

•

Joe Feczko, Christina Beem, Martine Reardon,
Ronnie Taffet, and Ritu Ahuja at Macy's

•

Lizzie Grubman Public Relations

•

Designers Management Agency

•

and Chronicle Books

HUGS  KISSES